Three Simple Questions

to Help Children Know God

Daphna Flegal

Abingdon Press

Nashville

Three Simple Questions

ISBN: 9781426742620

PACP00993282-01

Daphna Flegal lives in Nashville where she is a writer and editor of children's curriculum resources. She is a diaconal minister in West Michigan Conference of The United Methodist Church, where she served in local congregations as Director of Children's Ministries and Director of Christian Education. She presently serves as lead editor for children's resources at The United Methodist Publishing House. She is most excited about her newest job—grandmother.

Art: pp. 21–23, 43, 62–63 Megan Jeffery; p. 24 Randy Wollenann;
pp. 40–41 Robert S. Jones; p. 92 Brenda Gilliam

11 12 13 14 15 16 17 18 19 20—10 9 8 7 6 5 4 3 2 1

Printed in the U. S. A.

CONTENTS

Your church can do a churchwide study of the three simple questions by using the youth resource, *Three Simple Questions for Youth*, and the adult resource, *Three Simple Questions: Knowing the God of Love, Hope, and Purpose*, along with *Three Simple Questions to Help Children Know God*.

Churchwide Study and Intergenerational Activities

To help your congregation explore the ideas in Rueben P. Job's book *Three Simple Questions*, six-week studies are available for three age levels, so that you can create a churchwide program.

Adults
- *Three Simple Questions*, by Rueben P. Job
- DVD with Leader Guide

Youth
- *Three Simple Questions for Youth*

Children
- *Three Simple Questions to Help Children Know God*

As you study *Three Simple Questions* with the adults, youth, and children of your congregation, you may want to plan for group involvement in intergenerational activities. Consider these possibilities:

1. Plan a concluding celebration on a Sunday morning that will create a renewed commitment to asking and answering the basic questions of our faith. Recruit adults, youth, and children to offer testimonies about what they learned and practiced during their study.

2. Add an intergenerational activity to each session. For example, the combined group might create a group banner for each of the three simple questions. The banners can then be displayed in the sanctuary during the worship service as a reminder of what the groups have learned.

3. Make suggestions of songs or hymns that reflect the three simple questions for those who plan the worship services for the weeks following the study. Ask someone to name the connections to the three simple questions when the songs are sung.

4. Prepare a video or skits that illustrate the three simple questions. Involve actors from all age groups.

5. Have children, youth, and adults work together to design the worship altar that reflects the meanings of the three simple questions in the lives of Christians.

A Letter to the Early Christians

Dear friends, let's love each other, because love is from God. When we love each other it shows that we truly know God. Anyone who doesn't love others doesn't really know God, because God is love.

God showed us love when God sent Jesus into the world to give us life. This is love: it is not that we loved God but that God loved us so much that he sent his Son to us.

Dear friends, if God loved us this way, we should love each other. No one has ever seen God. If we love each other, God is always with us, showing us how to love like God loves.

The Elder

(Based on 1 John 4:7-12)

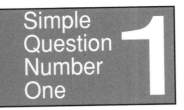

Who Is God?

First Week: God Is Love

Second Week: Jesus Teaches Us About God

Objectives

The children will

● discover that God is love;

● learn that as Christians we come to know God through the life and teachings of Jesus;

● recognize that because God loves us, we should love one another.

Bible Story

Week 1—1 John 4:7-12: God is love.

Week 2—John 3:16: God so loved the world.

Bible Verse

1 John 4:8: God is love.

Focus for the Teacher

Three Simple Questions

Our identity is found and formed by the God we worship and serve. Our life together as Christians is discovered, held together, and lived out based on our understanding of the God we have come to know and seek to follow.

Reflecting on the following three simple questions can lead us to a new and fuller understanding about who God is, who we are as individuals, and who we are together as Christians and as God's human family.

Who is God?

Who am I?

Who are we together?

These questions are not new; they are questions that Jesus himself faced and answered. Then he taught and lived those answers to and with his disciples and the crowds who followed.

Now, through the presence and power of the Holy Spirit, we can be taught the profound truth revealed by these simple questions for ourselves and for our time. Let's begin with the first question: **Who Is God?**

God Is Love

The Bible is filled with passages about a God who is best described and experienced as love.

Be mindful of your mercy, O LORD, and of your steadfast love, for they have been from of old. Do not remember the sins of my youth or my transgressions; according to your steadfast love remember me, for your goodness' sake, O LORD! (Psalm 25:6-7, NRSV).

I took them up in my arms; but they did not know that I healed them. I led them with cords of human kindness, with bands of love. I was to them like those who lift infants to their cheeks. I bent down to them and fed them (Hosea 11:3b-4, NRSV).

Beloved, let us love one another, because love is from God; everyone who loves is born of God and knows God. Whoever does not love does not know God, for God is love (1 John 4:7-8, NRSV).

As the Father loved me, I too have loved you. Remain in my love (John 15:9).

Therefore, imitate God like dearly beloved children. Live your life with love, following the example of Christ, who loved us and gave himself for us (Ephesians 5:l-2a).

It is clear from the experiences of the prophets and poets, Jesus, the apostles, and all the saints that have followed them—as well as from your experience and mine—that this way of love is neither easy nor strongly supported by our culture. It is a costly way, but also a deeply rewarding way.

It is costly because we will find ourselves at odds with our culture and its practice of using violent words and acts to settle issues and to attempt to carve out "safety" assumed to be found in confrontation and violence.

It is rewarding because there is the inner confirmation that it is the way of Jesus and the way for those who seek to follow him. And it is rewarding to experience the power of love in our lives and the impact of that way of love in the lives of others.

Jesus Is the True Image of God

Jesus gives us the clearest picture of who God is, what God does, and how God invites us to live as God's children.

- Jesus reveals a God who is author and creator of all things.

- In Jesus we see a God who reverses the values of our culture.

- In Jesus we see bold and radical truth.

- In Jesus we see a God who does the unexpected and the unpredictable.

- In Jesus we see a God who is not swayed by popular opinion.

- In Jesus we see a God who is not controlled by any ideology, philosophy, concept, or power.

- In Jesus we see a God who is never under our control but a God who is always free of any control and may act and create, as it seems wise and in keeping with God's will.

- In Jesus we see a God who is always and forever beyond us, completely other than we are, and yet Jesus tells us, a God who wants to come and dwell within us.

- In Jesus we see a God of love.

—adapted from *Three Simple Questions* by Rueben P. Job

> **Jesus gives us the clearest picture of who God is, what God does, and how God invites us to live as God's children.**
>
> **— Rueben P. Job**

The First Question for Children

Children begin their encounter with God through experience. A child can discover that God is love when he or she is surrounded by adults who model that love. Hopefully this begins even before birth as the child's parents prepare to welcome him or her into the family. And again, hopefully, the parents are surrounded by the love and support of others.

Unfortunately this is not always the case. Some children are not joyously welcomed, and some parents do not have a support system. This is where the church family can step in. Children can experience God's love modeled in worship, Sunday school, vacation Bible school, children's choirs, church sports, and the myriad of children's programs offered by churches.

Children can also experience God's love through caring adults who take the time to mentor children as they grow and seek the answers to these three simple questions.

This study is an opportunity for you to be a model of God's love. The Bible stories will teach the children about a loving God and the ways Jesus reveals God to us, but they will "catch" God's love through you. Thank you for helping children discover who God is.

First Week: God Is Love

Gather to Explore

Be sure that adult leaders are waiting when the first child arrives. Greet and welcome each child and involve him or her in an activity that introduces the theme for the day's activities.

Who Loves You?

- As the children arrive, give each child a heart that you have traced onto construction paper. Let each child cut out the heart. Precut the hearts for younger children.

- Encourage each child to draw a picture of someone who loves him or her. This might be a family member or friend. Older children may prefer to write the names of every person they can think of who loves them. Encourage them to fill the heart with names.

- *Ask*: Who is the person you drew on your heart? How do you know that person loves you? What does that person do to show you love?

- Encourage each child to tell you about his or her drawing.

- The children will use these hearts in the "Who Do You Love?" activity.

Prepare

✓ Use the smaller heart shape (page 20) to trace a heart onto construction paper for each child. Cut out the hearts for younger children.

✓ Provide crayons or markers and safety scissors.

Who Do You Love?

- Give each child a second heart tracing. Let each child cut out the heart. Precut the heart for younger children.

- Encourage each child to draw a picture of someone who loves him or her. This might be a family member or friend. Again, older children may prefer writing names on their hearts.

- *Ask*: Who is the person you drew on your heart? Is it the same person you drew on your first heart? Is it someone different? How do you show your love to that person?

- Encourage each child to tell you about his or her drawing.

- Instruct each child to stack the two hearts with the drawings facing out. Help each child staple around the edge of the hearts, leaving an opening on one side.

- Show the children how to crumple tissues or recycled newspapers and then stuff the paper into the hearts through the opening.

- Staple the opening closed.

- Use a paper punch to punch a hole in the top of each stuffed heart.

- Tie a loop of yarn or ribbon through the hole to make a hanger.

- Save the hearts to use with the "Snail Mail" game (see page 11).

Prepare

✓ Use the smaller heart shape (page 20) to trace a heart onto construction paper for each child. Cut out the hearts for younger children.

✓ Provide the hearts made in "Who Loves You?" along with crayons or markers, safety scissors, tissues or recycled newspaper, stapler and staples, a paper punch, and yarn or

Three Simple Questions to Help Children Know God

God Loves You!

- *Say*: There is someone else who loves each one of us. In fact, this someone loves everyone in the whole world.

- *Ask*: Can you guess who that is? (*God.*)

- Show the children the two larger hearts you have cut from construction paper. Write the name *God* in the center of each heart.

- Divide the children into two groups. Give each group a heart. Let each group work together to decorate its heart with crayons or markers.

- Help each group staple and stuff its heart. Add a loop of yarn to create the hanger and hang the larger heart in your room.

Love Squared

- Give each child a copy of the puzzle. Ask them to find, circle, and count how many times the word *love* is written in the square (*32*). They can look across and down. All the letters must be together on one line.

- *Say*: Our Bible verse today says, "God is love" (1 John 4:8).

Love Letters

- Set out paper and pens or pencils.

- Encourage the children to write letters to their parents, telling them that they love them.

- Set out plain paper, washable paint, and feather quills. Show the children how to dip the pointed end of the quills into the paint and then mark the paint on the paper.

- *Say*: In Bible times there were no crayons or pencils or markers or e-mails. Quills or reeds were used as pens for writing. In our Bible we can read letters written by biblical people. We call these letters the *Epistles*. Today our Bible story comes from one of the Epistles.

- Help the children fold their letters like Bibletime letters. Tell each child to fold the paper in half lengthwise, in half lengthwise again, and in half lengthwise a third time to form a narrow strip.

- Then show the children how to fold the narrow strip into thirds.

- Finally, tie the folded paper with a string.

- *Say*: Along with tying string around the paper, the letter was sealed with wax. If the seal was broken, the person receiving the letter knew that someone else had opened the letter.

- Lightly pencil the child's name on the outside of the folded letters. Set aside the letters to give to parents.

Prepare

✓ Use the larger heart shape (page 20) to trace two hearts onto construction paper. Cut out the hearts.

✓ Provide crayons or markers, safety scissors, tissues or recycled newspaper, stapler and staples, and yarn or ribbon.

Prepare

✓ Photocopy "Love Squared" (page 21) for each child.

✓ Provide crayons or pencils.

Prepare

✓ Provide paper, pens or pencils, washable paint, feather quills, plastic containers, recycled newspapers, paint smocks, and string.

✓ Cover the table with newspapers. Pour washable paint into plastic containers. Give each child a paint smock to wear.

Look in the Bible

The Bible helps us discover the answers to the three simple questions.

The Game of Love

- Bring the children to the center of the room.

- *Say*: Let's play a game about love. I will ask one of you: "Who do you love?" Because we all love one another, the person I select will begin describing someone in our group. Don't make the clues too easy. The rest of the group will try to guess the person being described. As soon as you think you know who the person is, go and stand behind that person. You can change your mind once. When it looks like everyone has decided, the person who is talking will go and stand behind the individual she or he has been describing.

- Play the game until everyone has had a chance to be loved.

Who Is God?

- *Ask*: I wonder who God really is? How can we discover the answer to that question? (*ask the pastor or someone else at church, ask our parents or other family member, come to church, look in the Bible*)

- Hold up the Bible.

- *Say*: The Bible is a good place to go to find answers to that question.

- Ask the children to locate 1 John in their Bibles. Practice the skill of finding the New Testament if your children are unfamiliar with Bible skills. (*Since 1 John is near Revelation, go to the back of the Bible. Go backward until the children come to 1 John.*)

- *Ask*: Is 1 John in the Old Testament or the New Testament? (*New Testament*) What book comes right before the Book of 1 John? (*2 Peter*) What book comes right after 1 John? (*2 John*) What kind of book is 1 John? (*Letters*) How many letters are there altogether? (*21*) How many books of the Bible have the name John? (*four—the Gospel of John and 1–3 John*)

- Invite a guest to dress like a New Testament man and to visit your class to read the letter (page 5) from a scroll. Or, read it yourself from a scroll.

- *Ask*: What did this letter tell us about God? (*God is love.*) What do you think it means to say, "God is love"? (*God treats us in loving ways.*) What are some ways God shows love to us? (*by creating the world for us, by being with us all the time, by listening to our prayers, by making each one of us unique, by sending Jesus*)

Prepare

✓ Photocopy "A Letter to the Early Christians" (page 5).

✓ Make a scroll using brown wrapping paper or a paper bag. If you use a paper bag, cut the bottom off the bag and cut open one side. Crumple the paper and then smooth it out again to make it look old. Glue the photocopy of the letter onto the scroll.

✓ Invite a guest to dress like a New Testament man and to visit your class to read the letter from a scroll.

Fun With Scripture

- Gather the children to sit in a circle. Give each child a Bible. Ask the children to open their Bibles to 1 John 4:7-12.

- Instruct the first person to read the first word, "Dear." The second person reads the second word, "friends," and the third person reads the word, "let's." On the fourth word, and every time the word *love* is read, ask the entire class to stand and shout "LOVE!"

- Move around the circle with each person reading one word of the Bible passage. Whenever you read the word *love*, *loves*, or *loved*, everyone stands and shouts "LOVE," then the next person continues.

- If you have a group of nonreaders, read the verses yourself and ask the class to jump up and repeat the word *love* after you.

- *Ask*: How did God reveal God's love to us? (*through Jesus, God's Son*)

Prepare
✓ Provide CEB Bibles.

Snail Mail

- Divide the children into two teams. Ask the two teams to move to one side of the room.

- Children in each team should choose partners. Designate one of the partners as the head of the snail and the other partner as the body.

- Place two boxes or baskets on the floor on the opposite side of the room. Place half of the stuffed hearts in one box or basket and the remaining half of the stuffed hearts in the second box or basket.

- *Say*: Today's Bible story is from 1 John, a letter in the New Testament. Letters were important to the early Christians, but there was no post office in Bible times. Persons who wanted to send and receive mail used slaves or paid couriers. Those who could not afford slaves or couriers hoped that they could find a person who was traveling in the direction they wanted to send the letter. And since travel was very slow, the mail in those times moved even slower.

- *Ask*: How many of you have ever received a letter? Who was it from? Do any of you receive e-mail from friends or family? Which is faster: regular mail or e-mail?

- *Say*: Today we are going to deliver messages by "snail mail." Each set of partners in your team makes a snail. Ask the partners to squat down. The child who is the body of the snail holds onto the shoulders of the child who is the head of the snail. In that position each "snail" will move across the room, take a heart from the basket or box, and bring it back to the team.

- When all the snails have picked up their "heart mail," the game is over.

- After the game, help the children hang their hearts around the room.

Prepare
✓ Provide two boxes or baskets and the stuffed hearts made earlier.

A Simple Practice

Discover ways to put into practice what you and the children have learned about God. Choose ways that match the children's interests and the time and resources you have available.

Because Love Is From God

- *Say*: Our Bible story says, "Dear friends, let us love each other, because love is from God" (1 John 4:7).

- *Ask*: What are some ways we can love one another?

- Encourage the children to brainstorm different ways they can show love to one another. (*use kind words, smile, share food, share toys, say "I love you," hug someone, pray for one another, and so forth*)

- Write the children's ideas on a large sheet of paper or a markerboard.

- *Say*: These are all great ideas. Who are some of the people you love? Is it easy to show love in these ways to those people?

- *Ask*: Have you ever come across someone that you had a hard time liking, much less loving? What are some things you can do to show that person love?

- Add any additional ideas to the list.

- *Say*: Even if the person is someone we find it difficult to like, we can still show love to that person. We can use kind words, we can smile, and we can always pray. We can pray that God will help us show love for the person, and we also can pray that God will help the person know that God loves him or her.

- Give each child a piece of paper. Ask the child to write the words "God is love" in the middle of the paper. Then, instruct each child to draw a heart around the words.

- Now ask each child to draw a line extending from the heart, with a circle at the end of the line.

- *Say*: We are going to show love by praying. In the circle write the name of someone you want to pray for. It can be someone you find easy to love or someone you find hard to love. (Help younger children write the names.)

- *Say*: Now take the crayons and draw doodles around the heart and around the circle. The doodles can be lines, dots, more hearts and circles, or any other shapes or symbols. Use lots of different colors. While you are doodling, think of the person you named. Thank God for that person. Ask God to help that person know about God's love. If you wish, you may add more circles and more names.

- Play a CD of quiet music as the children doodle and pray.

- Ask the children to fold up their papers and set them aside to take home. They do not need to share their prayers with anyone else.

Prepare

✓ Provide a large sheet of paper or markerboard, markers, writing paper, crayons or colored pencils, a CD player, and a CD of quiet music.

A Simple Meal

- *Say*: Because God loves us, we not only show love to people we know but also to people we don't know.

- *Ask*: Who are some people in our town that we might not know but who still need our love? (*people who are homeless, people who do not have enough money to buy food or clothes, people who are sick, people who cannot leave their homes, people who have a new baby*) What are some ways we can show love to these people? (*share food, send cards, pray for them*)

- *Say*: Let's make a simple meal of soup in a jar to give to someone we don't know.

- Tell the children about the people who will receive the soup. (*a food pantry, someone who is not feeling well, or the mother of a newborn*)

- Ingredients for one jar of soup

  ¼ cup each: dried garbanzo beans; dried navy beans or lima beans; dried red kidney beans or pinto beans; dried whole or split peas
  3 tablespoons dried minced onion
  2 tablespoons whole-wheat berries
  2 tablespoons pearl barley
  2 tablespoons dried celery flakes
  2 teaspoons instant beef bouillon granules
  ½ teaspoon dried basil, crushed 1 bay leaf
  salt

- Let the children combine and mix all the ingredients in a bowl, then pour the mixture in a one-quart canning jar. Tightly cap the jar.

- You may choose to work together to fill one jar or provide enough ingredients for each child to fill a jar.

Prepare

✓ Provide ingredients for soup mix, mixing bowl and spoons, measuring spoons and cups, and 1-quart canning jars with lids.

Greeting Cards

- Decorate cards to go with the soup. If you chose not to make the soup jar, children can make cards to send to persons in the hospital or who cannot leave home.

- Give each child a piece of construction paper. Show the children how to fold the paper in half to make a card.

- Ask the children to decorate the front of the cards with hearts. The children may draw hearts with crayons or markers, cut hearts out of paper and then glue them onto the cards, and/or add heart stickers to the front. Encourage the children to design their own cards.

- Instruct the children to glue the soup directions on the inside of each card and to write the Bible verse, "God is love" (1 John 4:8) somewhere on the cards.

- Help each child punch a hole through a corner of the card. Thread some ribbon through the hole, wrap the ribbon around the neck of the jar, and tie securely.

Prepare

✓ Provide soup jars prepared earlier, construction paper, glue, heart stickers, ribbon, safety scissors, crayons, and a paper punch.

✓ Photocopy and cut out the directions for "Dried Soup Mix" (page 23).

Celebrate and Praise God

One way we help children know God is to offer them opportunities to worship and praise both as a group and individually.

Litany of Love

- Call the children together for a time of celebration and praise.

- *Say*: We know God loves each one of us and wants us to love others. Listen to a "Litany of Love." Each time you hear me say, "That's just the way God is," say the Bible verse, "God is love" (1 John 4:8).

It doesn't matter who you are,
Or where your family lives.
God loves everyone, everywhere.
That's just the way God is.
God is love.

God loves the baby, oh, so small.
God loves the mother too.
God loves the young man grown so tall.
God loves me and you.

It doesn't matter who you are,
Or where your family lives.
God loves everyone, everywhere.
That's just the way God is.
God is love.

God loves the girl with braids in her hair.
God loves her grandpa too.
God loves the boy in his motorized chair.
God loves me and you.

It doesn't matter who you are,
Or where your family lives.
God loves everyone, everywhere.
That's just the way God is.
God is love.

God loves the woman who speaks with her hands.
God loves her brother too.
God loves all people in every land.
God loves me and you.

It doesn't matter who you are,
Or where your family lives.
God loves everyone, everywhere.
That's just the way God is.
God is love.

Second Week: Jesus Teaches Us About God

Gather to Explore

Be sure that adult leaders are waiting when the first child arrives. Greet and welcome each child and involve him or her in an activity that introduces the theme for the day's activities. The J E S U S mural will be used in Celebrate and Praise God.

All About Jesus

- As the children arrive, give each child a copy of the word puzzle.

- *Ask*: How much do you know about Jesus? How many words can you find in this puzzle that tell something about Jesus?

- Post a word list if the children need hints (see margin).

- To make the puzzle more fun, enlarge a copy of the puzzle on a photocopier. To make it as large as possible, enlarge the page a section at a time, than tape the sections together. Or, use the puzzle as a guide and hand letter the puzzle on mural paper. Post the enlarged puzzle on a wall and let the children work together to find the words.

- *Say*: Jesus teaches us about God. Our Bible verse is, "God is love" (1 John 4:8). God showed us love when God sent Jesus into the world.

J E S U S

- Give each child a piece of plain paper and ask him or her to draw a favorite story about Jesus and to identify the story drawn.

- Then ask the children to cut out around their pictures and glue them onto a large sheet of paper to create a montage.

- When finished, assign each child a letter from the name *JESUS*. You can have more than one set of letters.

- Offer the following suggestions, but encourage the children to create their individual designs.

> Cut the letters out of wallpaper or gift-wrap.
> Tear the letters out of brown paper bags.
> Twist pieces of paper in shapes to create the letters.

- Instruct the children to glue the letters on the montage to spell *JESUS*. Spell the name *JESUS* as many times as the letters will allow.

- *Say*: Jesus teaches us about God. Our Bible verse is, "God is love" (1 John 4:8). God showed us love when God sent Jesus into the world.

- Display the JESUS mural in your worship area.

Prepare

✓ Photocopy the "All About Jesus" puzzle (page 22) for each child.

✓ Provide pencils.

✓ **Option:** Enlarge the puzzle and mount it on a wall. Provide crayons or markers.

Word List

Son of God	teacher
healer	alive
love	carpenter
kind	Emmanuel
Lord	Savior

Words go across, down, backwards, up, and diagonally.

Prepare

✓ Provide a large piece of paper, drawing paper, glue, safety scissors, crayons or markers, various types of paper (wallpaper and/or gift-wrap), and brown paper grocery bags.

Grand Slam

- Make a grid of the pictures on the floor, two pictures across and two pictures down. Arrange the pictures randomly on the grid.

- Designate a batter's box spaced about ten feet from the grid.

- Divide the children into baseball teams. Let each team select its name.

- Designate first, second, and third bases and a home plate in an open area of the room. Somewhere between the picture grid and home plate, mark off a pitcher's box.

- Let each team decide on a batting order and a pitcher when they are in the outfield. There will be no need for players in the outfield. Those persons can retrieve the newspaper ball or keep score.

- The object of the game is for the batter to use a plastic bat or cardboard tube to hit the newspaper ball so that it lands on one of the "Grand Slam" pictures. The ball is considered "on" that square if it touches the colored square in any way. If the ball touches two squares, the batter can choose either square or hit again.

- The pictures indicate the kind of hit the batter gets. If the batter hits the ball three times and the ball does not land anywhere on the grid, he or she strikes out. If the ball lands on a picture, then the batter (with the help of remaining team members) must provide certain information geared to that picture.

  > Manger: Tell something you know about Jesus.
  > Cross: Name a book of the Bible that tells about Jesus.
  > Bible: Repeat the Bible verse.
  > Jesus: Say another name for Jesus.

- *Say*: Jesus teaches us about God. Our Bible verse is, "God is love" (1 John 4:8). God showed us love when God sent Jesus into the world.

Alphabet Pass

- Gather the children to sit in a circle on the floor.

- *Say*: When Jesus walked upon the earth he did many things to teach people about God. He worked miracles, told stories about God's love, and helped people. What are some other things Jesus did?

  We are going to play a game about things that Jesus did. I'll start by saying, "When Jesus walked upon the earth, he … ." Then I'll add a word or phrase that starts with the letter "a," such as "ate bread" or "amazed people" or "always cared."

  The next person in the circle will say, "When Jesus walked upon the earth, he … ." This person will repeat what I said and then add a word or phrase that begins with the letter "b," such as "broke bread." The next person will add a "c" to the chain. If someone gets stuck, we all will work together to help.

Prepare

✓ Photocopy and cut out four copies of the "Grand Slam" pictures (page 23).

✓ Tape the "Grand Slam" pictures onto pieces of construction paper.

✓ Make a newspaper ball by loosely wadding up recycled newspaper and wrapping it with masking tape. Do not pack and wrap it too tightly.

✓ Provide a plastic bat or a sturdy cardboard tube.

Look in the Bible

The Bible helps us discover the answers to the three simple questions.

Good News

- *Ask* the children to open their Bibles to the Table of Contents.

- *Ask*: What are the two testaments we find in the Bible? *(Old Testament and New Testament)* Our Bible verse is from 1 John 4:8. Is 1 John in the Old Testament or New Testament? *(New Testament)* What kind of book is 1 John? *(Letters)*

- *Say*: First John 4:8 is part of a letter. Let's read more of the letter.

- Read 1 John 4:9 together.

- *Ask*: How does this verse tell us that God showed us love? *(by sending Jesus into the world)*

- *Say*: Let's look again at the Table of Contents.

- *Ask*: What are the names of the first four books in the New Testament? *(Matthew, Mark, Luke, John)*

- *Say*: These four books are called the *Gospels*. They are the only books in the Bible that record what Jesus did and taught during his ministry. The word *gospel* comes from the Anglo-Saxon word *godspell*, which means "good news." The Gospels tell the good news that Jesus taught us about God.

- *Ask*: Let's look at a well-loved Bible verse from one of the Gospels. This verse helps us understand what Jesus shows us about God.

- Ask the children to turn to John 3:16 and read the Scripture together.

- *Ask*: What does this verse tell us about God? *(God loves the world.)* How do we know God loves the world? *(God loves us so much that God sent us Jesus.)* How does that make you feel?

God So Loves the World

- Read the following story to the children. Ask the children to guess the missing words as you tell the story.

In the beginning God created the heavens and the _____ *(earth)*. God filled the _____ *(earth)* with living creatures. Then God created _____ *(people)*. God loved these people. They loved God, too, but sometimes they loved themselves more.

More and more people were born into God's world. More and more people turned away from God. This made God very ___ *(sad)*. "I will speak to them. I will show them how much I ____ *(love)* them," God said.

The people listened to prophets. They tried to live as God wanted them to live. But sometimes it was hard, and they would go back to their old ways.

✓ Provide Bibles. Be sure that every child can see a Bible, even if it means having two children share a Bible.

"What should I do?" God wondered. "I know. I will send someone who is like them. This person will live with them. This person will show them how much I ____ (*love*) them."

God gave the prophets a message: "A special person is coming." And the people waited. And _____ (*waited*). And _____ (*waited*).

Then one day it happened. Baby Jesus was born. Angels announced the good news, "Today your Savior is ____ (*born!*)"

Jesus grew to be a man. He taught people about God. Jesus showed them God's ____ (*love*).

But not everyone believed Jesus was God's Son. Jesus was put to death on a _____ (*cross*) and buried in a garden ____ (*tomb*). But on the third day, God raised Jesus from the dead.

God is more powerful than anything people can possibly imagine. God is stronger than death. God promises us that if we believe that Jesus is God's Son, then we will also be given a life that never ends. The life, death, and resurrection of Jesus shows us that God is ____ (*love*).

Jesus, This Is Your Life!

- Allow the children to take turns drawing cards. As each child draws a card, he or she should tell something about that part of Jesus' life and then place the card face-up on the table.

- Let the children work together to place the cards in the order in which the events occurred. Cards that show teaching or healing can be placed anywhere between Jesus' baptism and the Palm Sunday processional. Don't worry about the exact time each event took place.

Prepare
✓ Photocopy and cut apart the "Life of Jesus" cards (page 24).

✓ Place the cards face-down on a table.

A Simple Practice

Discover ways to put into practice what you and the children have learned about God. Choose ways that match the children's interests and the time and resources you have available.

Tell Me the Stories of Jesus

- Hand out construction paper and ask each child to fold his or her paper in half, then tape or staple the sides together to make a pouch.

- Encourage the children to recall their favorite stories about Jesus. Explain that each child should draw a picture of her or his story on the front of a pouch.

- Give each child two sets of "Life of Jesus" cards to put inside his or her pouch.

- *Say*: You have created a concentration game about the life of Jesus. Play the game with a friend and teach that friend about Jesus. By helping someone learn about Jesus, you are helping them learn about God.

Prepare
✓ Photocopy and cut apart two sets of the "Life of Jesus" cards (page 24) for each child.

✓ Provide construction paper, crayons or markers, and tape or stapler and staples.

Celebrate and Praise God

One way we help children know God is to offer them opportunities to worship and praise both as a group and individually.

Jesus Teaches Us About God

- Call the children together for a time of celebration and praise. Point out the JESUS mural that they made at the beginning of the lesson.

- Ask the children to look at the mural. Point to one of the story pictures.

- *Ask*: What story is this? (Let the child who drew that picture respond.)

- *Say*: When Jesus (describe the story; for example, you might say, "When Jesus was born ... or When Jesus was baptized ..."), he taught us about God.

Sing the Bible Verse

- Ask all the children to say the Bible verse, "God is love" (1 John 4:8) together.

- Continue until each child has had an opportunity to tell about his or her picture on the mural.

- Sing the Bible verse using the words printed below. The tune is "God Is So Good."

> First John 4:8,
> First John 4:8,
> First John 4:8,
> Tells me, "God is love."
>
> Jesus, God's Son,
> Jesus, God's Son,
> Jesus, God's Son,
> Taught us, "God is love."
>
> We show our love,
> We show our love,
> We show our love,
> Because, "God is love."

- *Pray*: Thank you, God, for all the ways you show love to us. Thank you for your Son, Jesus, the greatest gift of love. Amen.

Prepare

✓ Provide the J E S U S mural made earlier (see page 15).

Three Simple Questions to Help Children Know God

Love Squared

LOVELOVELOV
OVELOVELOVE
VELOVELOVEL
ELOVELOVELO
LOVELOVELOV
OVELOVELOVE
VELOVELOVEL
ELOVELOVELO
OVELOVELOVE

All About Jesus

```
B Q U A R R Z Y S Z
D R E X D E D H B Z
A O M Q T T L R W E
L I M K W N Q A O P
I V A Z P E C M E L
V A N W J P N F O H
E S U Z J R Z V U L
X R E H C A E T Y J
R L L R H C D N I K
W L S O N O F G O D
```

Three Simple Questions to Help Children Know God

Grand Slam

Dried Soup Mix

In a large saucepan, combine contents of this jar with 7 cups water. Bring to boiling and reduce heat. Simmer for 2 minutes. Remove from heat, cover, and let stand 1 hour. (Or soak bean mixture in the water overnight in a covered pan.) Do not drain. After standing 1 hour, bring beans and liquid to boiling and reduce heat. Cover and simmer 1½ to 2 hours or until beans are tender. Remove bay leaf. Season to taste. Makes 6 to 8 servings.

This soup is shared with you by the children of _____

Life of Jesus

Three Simple Questions to Help Children Know God

Mirror Messages

Turn around three times and then touch the floor.	Clap your hands twice and then hop on one foot.
Tap your nose one time. Then put your hands on your hips.	Touch your head, your shoulders, and your toes.
Smile in the mirror and say, "God loves me!" three times.	Stretch your arms up as high as you can. Now jump!
Touch each elbow. Then touch each knee. Tap your toes.	Shake one leg. Shake the other leg. Do the hokey-pokey.

Simple Question #2: Who Am I?

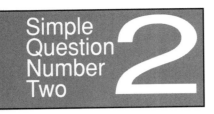

Simple Question Number Two **2**

Who Am I?

First Week: Made in God's Image
Second Week: A Beloved Child of God

Objectives

The children will
- discover what it means to be made in God's image;
- recognize themselves as children of God;
- realize that because we are God's children we can talk to God anytime and anywhere about anything.

Bible Story

Week 1—Genesis 1:26-31: God creates human beings.
Week 2—1 John 3:1-2: We are God's children.

Bible Verse

Genesis 1:27: God created humanity in God's own image.

Focus for the Teacher

Who Am I?

There is an old Sunday school song that says, "If anybody asks you who I am, tell them I'm a child of God." This is the answer we want our children to discover for themselves as they grow in their relationship with God and with the family of faith. And, with the realization that they are indeed children of God, we want our children to acknowledge that all people around the world are also children of God.

In the Beginning

A first step in accepting ourselves as children of God is to look at the Creation. The Creation story in Genesis is so much more than a step-by-step record of the appearance of life on earth. This Scripture is a celebration of human beings—made in the image of God—as the completion of God's plan of creation.

Humans are different from any of the other living creatures. They share the spiritual characteristics of God that no other creature shares. Humans can think, remember, make plans for the future, choose, create, and reflect on their experiences. Human beings rise above their animal instincts for personal survival to care about the survival of others. Humans are spiritual beings. They can worship God and can experience feelings of awe and wonder. They can appreciate God's world and can live in fellowship with God, who is Spirit, and with other human beings. Like no other creatures, humans can pray to God and receive and understand God's answers.

In God's Image

When we talk about the image of God, we need to consider more than physical characteristics. Although the image of God is partly physical, because the body is part of being a whole person, it also includes the spiritual, emotional, and intellectual aspects of human beings. We exist as body and soul together.

Humans are a mirror of God to the world. We reflect God's characteristics, but we are not God. And so the question we need to ask ourselves is: "When people see me, do they see God?"

In the ancient cultures of the Near East, the king was considered to be the representative of God on earth. Egyptians thought of their pharaohs as images of God living on the earth. In the Genesis account, this holy responsibility is given not just to kings but to every human—both male and female. As images of God and stewards of God's creation, we have the responsibility of making sure that God's plan for creation is fulfilled.

Children of God

God has made us children through God's self-giving love. We have done nothing to deserve God's love. It just is. We are children of God. This realization can change our view of ourselves.

Rueben Job writes in *Three Simple Questions:* "Whenever he was troubled or dismayed, the reformer Martin Luther would remember his baptism. Roland Bainton writes in *Here I Stand: A Life of Martin Luther:* 'Luther attached great importance to his baptism. When the Devil assailed him, he would answer I am baptized' (Abingdon Press, 1950; page 367).

"Remembering his baptism reassured Luther that he was a beloved child of God, that no threat could frighten him, and that no power could snatch him from the loving arms of God.

"Those familiar with Luther's custom have found a practice of their own to remind themselves who they are, and it is something that can be practiced by all Christians. The practice is simply to speak your own name, put your fingers to your head, and repeat, 'Remember who you are.' As you do this, remember your baptism and affirm that you are a beloved child of God. Then offer a prayer of thanks. This simple practice can be a reassuring reminder of who we are as children of God."

The realization that we are children of God also changes our view of the world. It causes us to affirm all the people we see around us as children of God—which makes them our brothers and sisters. And, as brothers and sisters, they must not be labeled as less than children of God because they have a different theological position, lifestyle, or worldview than our own.

Who Am I? for Children

Children are forming self-images that will be with them all their lives. Created in God's image is an important message for your children.

> **We were made in God's image, and God chooses to dwell within us.**
> — Rueben P. Job

When children picture God in their minds, they probably imagine something akin to the Sistine Chapel and Michaelangelo's vision of God. (At the very least God will look old with long hair and a beard.) So, to them, the term *image of God* probably means "looking like God." But if we are all created in "God's image," how can we all look like God? Even the children will see the improbability of this concept. In today's session we will help the children move beyond the outside image to the inside image. It is our "inside self" that reflects God in our lives. It is our inside self that relates to God and to other people. It is our inside self that possesses those spiritual gifts that help us reflect God in the world today.

As children grow they become more concerned about their image. How do they look? Are they saying and doing the right things to gain acceptance? They may worry about challenges they face in school, sports, or in surviving the neighborhood. Assure your children that they are God's special creation, loved and valued by God.

It is important to help children develop positive self-images. Teachers have many opportunities to affirm children. Make it a point to emphasize their uniqueness. Listen to them. Give them your full attention. Get down on their level and look in their faces. Accept their thoughts and feelings. Constantly remind them that they are loved. Model God's love through your actions and words. Constantly "catch" your children doing things right.

As children grow into their elementary years, they begin to identify with the group that affirms them and makes them feel good. This is an opportunity to help your children identify themselves as Christian. Through our faith as adults, and through our beliefs and actions as Christians, we pass on the faith. This is also an opportunity for your church to pass down the special heritage of your denomination. But more importantly, it is an opportunity to help the children see themselves as children of God.

Gather to Explore

Be sure that adult leaders are waiting when the first child arrives. Greet and welcome each child and involve him or her in an activity that introduces the theme for the day's activities. The "Self-portraits" will be used again in the A Simple Practice *section.*

Reflection Stations

- Choose from the following activities and set up two or more Reflection Stations. If possible decorate the Reflection Stations area with mirrors.

- Each of the activities included in the Reflections Stations uses mirrors. If possible provide a mirror for each child. If this is not possible, you can use one mirror in each activity and the children can take turns.

Mirror Messages

- Give each child one of the "Mirror Messages."

- *Say*: Each of you has a message. This message tells you to do something. Try to read the message and do what it says.

- After a few minutes, show the children how to hold the messages in front of a mirror. The children will be able to read the messages by looking in the mirror. Let the children do what the messages say to do.

- *Ask*: When you look in a mirror, what do you see? (*a reflection of an object*)

- *Say*: A mirror works because it is a smooth, shiny surface that receives the light from an object and reflects it back to your eyes. We call what you see in the mirror an "image." A mirror produces a clear image of the object that's in front of it because the light is reflected in a straight line.

- *Say*: Today we're talking about what it means to be created in God's image. We all are like mirrors, reflecting God back to the world.

Mirror Play

- Let the children experiment with hand mirrors. Encourage the children to hold the mirrors so that they can look behind themselves, try to look around a corner, and look over a wall.

- Ask a child to sit underneath a table. Place an object on top of the table and let the child use a mirror to identify the object while staying under the table.

- *Say*: Today we're talking about what it means to be created in God's image. We all are like mirrors, reflecting God back to the world.

Prepare

✓ Photocopy and cut apart the "Mirror Messages" (page 25).

✓ Provide a mirror.

Prepare

✓ Provide hand mirrors.

Mirror Madness

- Let the children choose partners. Instruct each child to draw a simple shape (square, circle, or triangle) on a sticky note and then place the sticky note on the back of his or her partner.

- Let the children take turns using mirrors to learn what shapes have been drawn on the stickies on their backs.

- *Say*: Mirrors reflect images. Today our Bible verse says that "God created humanity in God's own image" (Genesis 1:27). We are a reflection of God.

- *Ask*: Do you think that verse means that we look like God? (*no*) How do we reflect God? (*by how we act*) What are some ways people can reflect God? (*love others, be kind, take care of the world*)

Prepare

✓ Provide mirrors, sticky notes, and pens or pencils.

Self-portraits

- Show the children self-portraits by Van Gogh and other artists.

- *Ask*: Which self-portrait do you like the best? Why?

- *Say*: Artists often use mirrors to draw their self-portraits. One famous artist, Vincent Van Gogh, painted 22 self-portraits.

- *Say*: Today our Bible verse says that we are created in God's image.

- *Ask*: What do you think that statement means?

- Give each child drawing paper, a pencil, and a mirror. (Or, provide enough mirrors for the children to easily share.)

- *Say*: Look at your face in the mirror. Where are your eyes positioned? They are in the middle, between the bottom of your chin and the top of your forehead. The width across your face measures five eyes wide.

  Now look at your nose. Where is the bottom of your nose? It is halfway between your eyes and the bottom of your chin.

  Now look at where your mouth is positioned. It is in the middle of your face, between the bottom of your nose and your chin. Notice the width of your mouth. Your mouth is as wide as the pupils (black dot in each eye) in your eyes.

  Now look at your ears. Where do the top of your ears begin? The ears start at the same level as the eyebrows. Where do the bottoms of your ears end? The ears stop at the same level as the bottom of the nose.

- Let the children color their self-portraits with crayons or colored pencils.

- Save the self-portraits to use during the *A Simple Practice* activities (see "Add to Your Self-portrait" on page 32.

Prepare

✓ Provide mirrors, drawing paper, pencils, and crayons or colored pencils.

✓ Provide a copy of *Self-Portrait with Straw Hat* by Vincent Van Gogh as well as self-portraits from other well-known artists such as Rembrandt and Norman Rockwell. Search online or in the library for images of the paintings.

Look in the Bible

The Bible helps us discover the answers to the three simple questions.

Mirror Movements

- Allow the children to choose partners. Instruct partners to stand facing each other.

- *Say*: We have been looking in mirrors. Now let's try being mirrors.

- Instruct the partners to choose one person to be the leader while the second person acts as the mirror. Ask the leader to begin slowly moving his or her arms and hands. The person acting as the mirror must try to exactly duplicate the leader's movements.

- After a few minutes, tell the partners to switch roles.

- *Say*: Today we're talking about what it means to be created in God's image. We are all like mirrors, reflecting God back to the world.

In God's Image

- *Ask*: Have you ever wondered why you are the way you are? Maybe you don't like tomatoes, even though everyone else in your family does. Or maybe you are really good at sports but your brother is really good at music. Or maybe you like to talk a lot, but your best friend is shy and quiet. Have you ever looked at yourself in the mirror and asked, "Who am I?"

- Hold up the Bible.

- *Say*: The Bible has an answer to that question.

- Ask the children to find and read together Genesis 1:26-31.

- *Ask*: What did God create? (*humanity, humans*) How did God create humanity? (*in God's image*) What did God create as humanity? (*male and female*) What did God think about Creation? (*very good*)

- *Say*: This Scripture is a celebration of human beings as the magnificent completion of God's plan of creation. Of all God's creations, only human beings—made in the image of God—were pronounced "very good" by God.

- Tell or read the story "In God's Image."

- *Ask*: What does it mean when we say that we are made in God's image? (*Invite the children to talk about their feelings and thoughts.*)

- *Say*: God created human beings who could think about and make decisions, design and build new things, anticipate problems and work out solutions, share ideas with one another, love and care for one another, and enjoy all that God had created. In other words, God created human beings to be like God.

Prepare

✓ Photocopy "In God's Image" (page 39).

Fun With Scripture

- Gather the children to sit in a circle around the teacher.

- Repeat the Bible verse together several times: "God created humanity in God's own image" (Genesis 1:27).

- The teacher will then call out a category, such as "blue eyes." Other categories might include: brown eyes, curly hair, straight hair, wears glasses, does not wear glasses, has a pet, and does not have a pet.

- Everyone with blue eyes should stand and say the Bible verse together.

- From time to time the teacher should call out, "It was very good," and the whole class should stand and say the verse together.

Scripture Search

- Assign the children to small groups. If you have a variety of ages, mix younger and older children together. If you have a small class, all the children can work together in one group. Make sure each group has a Bible.

- *Say*: Let's search the Scriptures to discover how the Bible describes God.

- Give each group one piece of black construction paper and one piece of white construction paper.

- Each group should choose someone in its group to cut off one-half inch around each edge of the white construction paper, making the white construction paper smaller than the black construction paper.

- Each group should then choose another person in its group to glue the white construction paper on top of the black construction paper, leaving a black frame around the white paper. (This is a good activity for the youngest member of the group.)

- A third person in each group should fold the papers in half, with the white paper on the inside and the black paper on the outside, simulating a "Bible."

- Depending on the size of your class, give each group two or three Scripture passages to look up and read. The older children will need to help the younger children find and read the verses.

- After reading the Scriptures, each group should choose a recorder to write in its "Bible" how God is described by the Scriptures.

- Finally, each group should choose a reporter to tell what they have learned.

- *Say*: Since we are made in God's image, we possess these same characteristics.

- Display the "Bibles" around the room.

Prepare

✓ Photocopy and cut apart the "Scripture Search" references (page 40).

✓ Provide black and white construction paper, glue, thin markers, and safety scissors.

A Simple Practice

Discover ways to put into practice what you and the children have learned about God. Choose ways that match the children's interests and the time and resources you have available.

Add to Your Self-portrait

- Hand out the self-portraits made earlier. Instruct the children to glue their self-portraits onto construction paper.

- Now hand out the "Add to Your Self-portrait" pages, one per child. Instruct the children to cut out the words and pictures. Precut the words and pictures for younger children.

- Help the children read the words and identify the pictures. Define the words and talk about the characteristics the pictures represent (*heart = loving; smile = happy; mad face = angry; shaking hands = friendly*).

- Ask the children to choose pictures and words that they think reflect those characteristics in God's image that we would like to see in ourselves.

- Encourage the children to glue the chosen words and pictures around their self-portraits on the construction paper.

Three Very Short Stories

- *Say*: In today's Bible story we learn that human beings were created in the image of God. We've looked at mirrors and talked about ways that we reflect God. Now I'm going to read three very short stories. If the person in the story is reflecting the image of God, say, "It was very good." If the person in the story is not reflecting the image of God, stay silent.

- Read the following scenarios to the children.

  1. Ben is playing basketball in his driveway when he sees his elderly neighbor struggling to drag her trash can to the side of the road. He stops playing basketball and runs to help her. (*It was very good.*)

- *Ask*: Ben is reflecting the image of God. What characteristic of God do we see in Ben? (*being kind or loving*)

  2. Sarah sees the new girl, Abby, coming towards the lunch table where Sarah is sitting with her friends. Sarah quickly puts her backpack on the empty chair next to her. When Abby tries to sit with Sarah and her friends, Sarah says, "You can't sit here; this seat is taken." (*stay silent*)

  3. Sarah sees the new girl, Abby, coming towards the lunch table where Sarah is sitting with her friends. Sarah quickly pulls out the empty chair next to her. "Come sit here," Sarah says to Abby, "You can eat lunch with us." (*It was very good.*)

- *Ask*: Sarah is reflecting the image of God. What characteristic of God do we see in Sarah? (*being friendly*)

Prepare

✓ Photocopy "Add to Your Self-portrait" (page 40) for each child. Cut out the words and pictures for younger children.

✓ Provide the self-portraits made earlier, construction paper, glue, and safety scissors.

Celebrate and Praise God

One way we help children know God is to offer them opportunities to worship and praise both as a group and individually.

God, Help Me to Be…

- Children will prepare "God's Earth" ball for the closing celebration.

- Choose one or more children to color the two earth pictures with crayons or markers and then cut out the pictures.

- Staple together the two earth pictures with the colored sides facing out. Leave an opening along one edge.

- Instruct the children to crumple tissues or recycled paper into small balls. Stuff the crumpled paper into the earth pouches, staple the opening closed, and cover the staple prongs with tape.

- Ask the children to sit or stand in a circle.

- Hold up the completed earth ball for the children to see.

- *Say*: This ball reminds us of all that God created—the sky, the sea, the land, and all the living things. We know that on the sixth day of Creation, after God created the animals, God created human beings. And God made these human beings in the image of God. Sometimes our actions are not good reflections of what God is like. So, today, let's ask God to help us live in God's image.

  I will toss the earth ball to one of you. You'll say, "God, help me to be …" and then name something that will reflect the image of God. For example, you might say, "Help me to be more patient," or "Help me to be more kind." Then you will toss the ball back to me.

- Toss the ball to the first person and encourage him or her to make the statement and then toss the ball back to you. Continue tossing the earth ball until everyone has had an opportunity to talk.

Affirm the Children

- Ask the children to sit or stand in a circle.

- Touch one of the children on his or her shoulders.

- *Say*: Today I praise God for (*name the child*), who is made in the image of God.

- Continue around the circle, naming each child and leader.

- *Pray*: Thank, you, Great Creator, for all your children. Amen.

Prepare

✓ Photocopy two copies of "God's Earth" (page 41).

✓ Provide crayons or markers, stapler and staples, masking tape, safety scissors, and tissues or recycled paper.

Gather to Explore

Be sure that adult leaders are waiting when the first child arrives. Greet and welcome each child and involve him or her in an activity that introduces the theme for the day's activities. The purpose of these beginning activities is to help children recognize that they are persons of worth simply because they are children of God. The "Coat of Arms" activity will be used again in the A Simple Practice *section. The "Fingerprints" activity will be used in the* Celebrate and Praise God *section.*

Hello, My Name Is…

- As the children arrive, give each child a copy of the name poster.

- Instruct the children to write their first names, putting one letter in each box down the left side of the paper.

- *Say*: Use the beginning letters to write a positive phrase or word that describes who you are. For example, if your name is Nina, the first word should begin with the letter "N," so you might write the word *nice* (see sample in margin).

- Encourage the children as they think of words to complete the activity. You may need to help younger children write their words.

- Instruct the children to draw a picture of themselves in the frame provided on the poster.

- Read aloud each child's words as you display the poster in the room.

- *Say*: Our Bible story tells us that God loves each one of us, and each one of us is a child of God.

Prepare

✓ Photocopy the "Hello, My Name Is …" poster (page 42) for each child.

✓ Provide crayons or markers and tape.

Hello, My name is …

Super
Artistic
Marvelous
and I'm a child of God!

Coat of Arms

- Give each child a "Coat of Arms" pattern. Older children may use the pattern to trace and cut out a coat of arms on poster board. Precut the coat of arms for younger children.

- Use the following instructions to help children draw a picture in each section of the coat of arms.

- Section 1: Draw a happy memory from one of your birthdays.
Section 2: Draw something you are good at doing.
Section 3: Draw something you have done that makes you proud.
Section 4: Draw something you want to do in your life, or draw what you want to be when you grow up.

- Display the coats of arms around the room. Plan to have the children talk about their coats of arms during the *A Simple Practice* section.

Prepare

✓ Photocopy the "Coat of Arms" (page 43) for each child.

✓ Provide poster board, paper, safety scissors, and crayons or markers.

Fingerprints

- Give each child a piece of plain paper. Let the children help one another trace their hands on the paper. Then instruct the children to add their thumb and fingerprints to the hand tracings.

- Show the children how to press their thumbs or fingers onto a nonpermanent ink pad and then onto their handprints. Children can use hand wipes to remove the ink from their fingers.

- Encourage the children to examine their fingertips with the magnifying glass. Point out the lines on their skin, then allow the children to examine their prints. Again, point out the lines.

- Ask children to cut out their handprints and save for use in the *Celebration and Praise God* section. You may need to help younger children cut out their handprints.

- *Say:* Everyone has different fingerprints. (*Allow the children to compare their prints.*) Each one of us is a unique child of God.

Prepare

✓ Provide plain paper, magnifying glasses, nonpermanent ink pads, safety scissors, and hand wipes.

Shake It!

- Ask the children to move to an open area of the room.

- *Say*: Each of us is a unique child of God. Each of us has his or her own name, fingerprints, and personality. Listen to the music. As the music plays, move around the room. When the music stops, quickly find a partner. Then do what I tell you to do.

- Play lively music and encourage the children to move around the room. Stop the music and allow the children to find partners.

- *Say*: One of you is partner A and the other is partner B. I want partner A to introduce him or herself to partner B. Partner A, look partner B in the eyes, shake his or her hand, and say, "Hi! My name is (*say your name*), and I'm a child of God." Partner B, answer, "Yes! You're a child of God." Then switch partners and do it again with partner B saying the introduction.

- Play the music again and repeat the exercise with new partners.

Prepare

✓ Provide a CD of lively music and CD player.

I Like Myself

- Ask the children to sit in a circle.

- *Say*: Let's play a game. To play this game you will need to think of something you like about yourself. For example you might think, *I like myself because I have a great smile*, or *I like myself because I'm a good soccer player*. Remember, just think it. Then, when I call your name, stand in the center of the circle and say, "I like myself because ...," then act out your thought. The rest of us will guess what you're acting out.

- Give each child a turn. The other children should clap and cheer for each child as he or she returns to sit in the circle.

Look in the Bible

The Bible helps us discover the answers to the three simple questions.

Give Your Opinion

- Ask the children to open their Bibles to 1 John 3:1-2.

- *Say*: Our Bible verses tell us that we are God's children. Listen to these verses from the Contemporary English Version of the Bible.

- Read 1 John 3:1-2 (CEV) to the children:

    Think how much the Father loves us. He loves us so much that he lets us be called his children, as we truly are. But since the people of this world did not know who Christ is, they don't know who we are. My dear friends, we are already God's children, though what we will be hasn't yet been seen. But we do know that when Christ returns, we will be like him, because we will see him as he truly is.

- *Say:* Let's think about what these verses mean.

- Point out the signs you posted in the room.

- Read each of the statements printed below, pausing briefly after each one. If the children agree with the statement, they should walk to the "Agree" side of the room. If they disagree with the statement, they should move to the "Disagree" area. They should go to the "Not Sure" area if they're unsure of their answers. Emphasize that there are no wrong answers.

    1. God's children love God.
    2. God loves brown-eyed children more than green-eyed children.
    3. I am God's child, and I am important to God.
    4. God's children are all alike.
    5. God's children are unique.
    6. You are God's child, and you are important to God.

Mirror Movements Plus

- Ask the children to choose partners and stand facing each other.

- Say the Bible verse together with the children: "God created humanity in God's own image" (Genesis 1:27).

- Instruct the partners to choose one person to be the leader, while the second person acts as the mirror. The leader should begin slowly moving his or her arms and hands. The person acting as the mirror must try to exactly duplicate the leader's movements.

- This is just like the activity on page 30 *except* that, as the partners move, they must recite the Bible verse.

- After a few minutes, allow the partners to switch roles.

Prepare

- ✓ Provide Bibles, construction paper, markers, and tape.

- ✓ Use the construction paper to make three signs: "Agree," "Disagree," and "Not Sure." Post the "Agree" sign on one side of the room. Post the "Disagree" sign on the opposite side of the room. Post the "Not Sure" sign in the middle.

A Simple Practice

Discover ways to put into practice what you and the children have learned about God. Choose ways that match the children's interests and the time and resources you have available.

Because We Are Who We Are

- *Ask*: After reading today's Bible verses, if I were to ask you, "Who are you?"—what would you answer?

- *Say*: Hopefully you would say, "I am a child of God, or I am made in God's image." And because we are children of God, we can talk to God anytime and anywhere.

- Read the poem printed in the margin. Encourage the children to pump their fists in the air and shout the word, "Yes!" after each phrase.

- Lead the children to brainstorm other times and places they can talk to God.

Prayer Race

- *Ask*: What do we call it when we talk to God? (*prayer*)

Say: Not only can we talk to God anytime and anywhere, but also we can talk to God about anything.

- Divide the children into two teams and instruct the teams to line up on one side of the room. Place a bell or whistle opposite each team.

- Read aloud one of the situations below. The teams must decide when, where, and how (alone, in a group, right where they are, and so forth) they could pray about that situation.

- When the team has made a decision, a chosen team member must run and ring the bell or blow the whistle. A different team member represents the team each time.

1. You are having a difficult time learning math.
2. Your grandmother is sick.
3. The news has reported a natural disaster that has destroyed a town in another country.
4. One of the older kids at school has been bullying you.
5. You are going to be moving far away.
6. You've had nightmares every night for two weeks.
7. You are going to be in a contest and you really want to win.
8. You and your best friend had a fight.
9. When you woke up this morning it was a perfect day for your favorite sport—and it's Saturday!
10. It's lunch time at school and you eat in the cafeteria.

Can you talk to God when you brush your teeth?
Yes!
Can you talk to God before going to sleep?
Yes!
Can you talk to God when you're feeling glad?
Yes!
Can you talk to God when you're feeling sad?
Yes!
Can you talk to God while you're at school?
Yes!
Can you talk to God as you float in the pool?
Yes!
Can you talk to God by singing a song?
Yes!
Can you talk to God all day long?
Yes!

Prepare

✓ Provide a bell or whistle for each team.

Celebrate and Praise God

One way we help children know God is to offer them opportunities to worship and praise both as a group and individually.

Joys and Concerns

- Display two large sheets of paper in your celebration area. Write the word *joys* on one piece of paper and the word *concerns* on the second piece of paper.

- *Ask*: How was your past week? Did anything happen to you or someone you know that was fun or that you think is a good thing?

- Tell something good that happened to you. Write it on the "joy" page.

- Encourage the children to name the good things that have happened to them, their friends, and their families. List what they share on the "joy" page.

- *Ask:* Are you worried about anything? Is someone you know sick? Did something happen this week that caused people to be hurt?

- Encourage the children to name their concerns. List whatever they share on the "concern" page.

- *Say*: Now I am going to lead us in a prayer litany. When I point to the group say, "God, hear our prayer."

- *Pray*: Dear God, we know we are your children, and we can talk to you anytime and anywhere. Thank you for listening to us whenever we talk to you. Right now we are concerned about ... (*name the concerns listed in groups; for example, all those who are sick*).

- Point to the children and have them say, "**God, hear our prayer.**"

- *Continue to pray:* God, we thank you for ... (*name the joys listed*).

- Point to the children and have them say, "**God, hear our prayer.**"

Our Affirmation

- Place a large piece of poster board on a table.

- Hand out glue and instruct the children to glue "Our Affirmation" onto colored construction paper and then onto the poster board.

- Give the children their handprint cutouts and tell them to glue their handprints around "Our Affirmation," being careful not to cover the words.

- Display the poster in your celebration area.

- Gather the children around the "Our Affirmation" poster and read it together.

- *Pray*: God, you have created us in your image and made us your children. Thank you. Amen.

Prepare

✓ Provide two large sheets of paper, markers, and tape.

Prepare

✓ Photocopy "Our Affirmation" (page 44).

✓ Provide the handprint cutouts made earlier, glue, colored construction paper, and a large piece of poster board.

In God's Image

by Michael E. Williams

A long time ago teachers, called rabbis or sages, told stories to help people understand different passages of Scripture. These stories were called *midrashim* (or *midrash*, if only one such story). They were often included in sermons or lessons and then later were recorded and passed down. This story is based upon a *midrash* about Creation.

When God began to create, it was as if God told a story that became the universe. As soon as the words rolled off God's tongue, they became the very things they described. When God said "light," there was light. When God said "land," there was land. When God said "sun, moon, and stars," these lights began to dance around the heavens. When God said "plants and animals," you know what happened. Everything that God spoke came to be.

When the story was nearly complete, God thought that there was something missing. Of all the characters of Creation, there was none creative enough to say that they were like God. In other words, there was not a creature who could tell a story back to God.

So God said, "Let us create a character who is like us. Let us create a character in the divine image."

Us! That's right. The original story has God speaking in plural. Who is us? The Bible doesn't say, but some of the ancient rabbis used their imaginations and guessed that God was talking to the heavenly host, the angels. And these rabbis suggest that the angels didn't like what they heard. They saw a danger in making a character who was too much like God, for that creature would have entirely too much freedom.

"If you create beings with so much freedom," said one angel, "then they will be free to create schools and universities and research institutes. They will invent microscopes and telescopes and will explore all the secrets of your Creation. Before long they will discover molecules and atoms and subatomic particles. They will find stars invisible to the ordinary eye. Even black holes and quarks will be no mystery to them. They will find the secrets you have woven into the fabric of the universe."

"So?" was God's only reply.

Another angel added to the warning: "You realize, don't you, that these creatures would soon discover medicines. Some would know what medicines to give for any ailment. Others would learn to open the body and repair its parts. Before long they would replace those parts with other body parts and even machines that they have invented. These creatures would live longer and longer until there is no telling how long they would live."

"Long life's not a bad thing, if it is lived well," was God's only reply.

One more angel spoke: "Creatures with so much freedom to be creative will soon learn to imitate you. They will be painting portraits of other creatures and of themselves. They will hear the sounds of your universe and put them together in different patterns, then call it music. They will move in imitation of the swaying of trees in the wind or the easy rolling walk of a cat on a stroll and call it dance. They will learn to tell and write stories and call it literature. They will act out those stories and call it theater."

"Don't you understand?" God interrupted. "That's the idea. They are supposed to be creative like I am creative. They are supposed to be playful like I'm playful. They are supposed to enjoy this wonder-filled story I have told as much as I do."

"But," added the angel in a last-ditch effort to talk God out of this plan, "what if they think of something you haven't thought of?"

At that God leaned back and let out a hearty laugh, pounding large divine hands against the chest from which emerged the heartbeat of the universe, and said with obvious delight: "Well, then, I'll just have to say that my children have done better than even I could do."

Then the rabbis say that God created human beings in God's image. Both males and females were created with the freedom to choose what God had dreamed of them becoming all along.

—adapted from *BibleZone 7* Older Elementary © 1999 Abingdon Press

Scripture Search

Psalm 100:5	Psalm 116:5
1 John 4:8	1 John 4:16
Isaiah 40:28	1 Samuel 16:7
Psalm 54:4	Numbers 14:20

Add to Your Self-portrait

Loving   Friendly

Angry   Happy

God's Earth

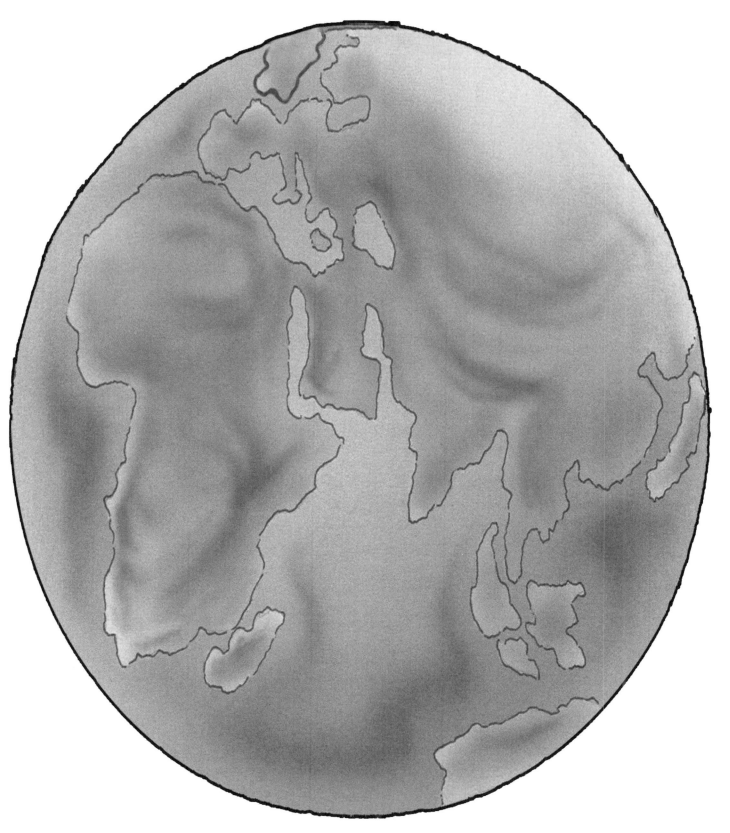

Hello, My Name Is...

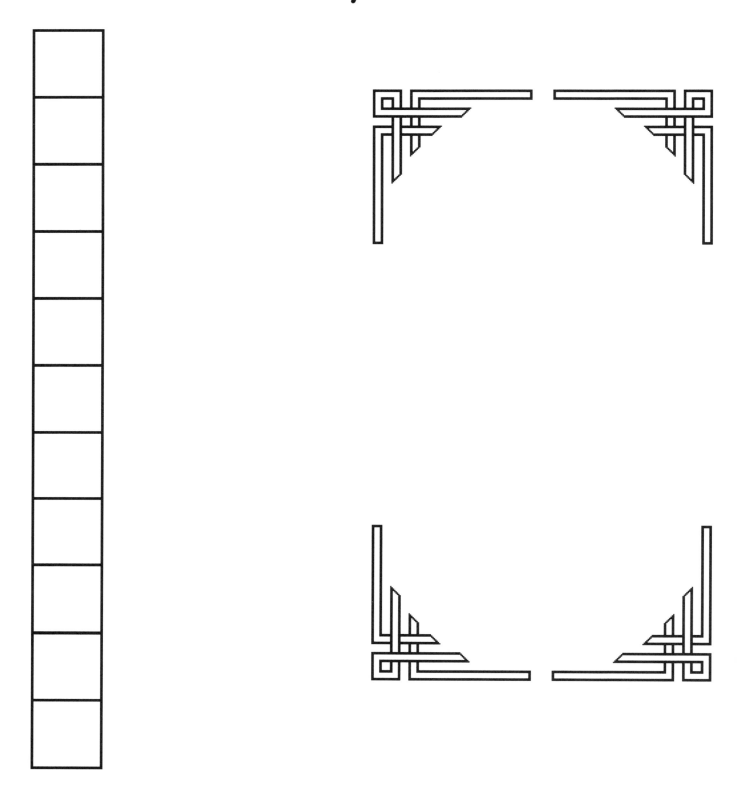

And I'm a child of God!

Three Simple Questions to Help Children Know God

Coat of Arms

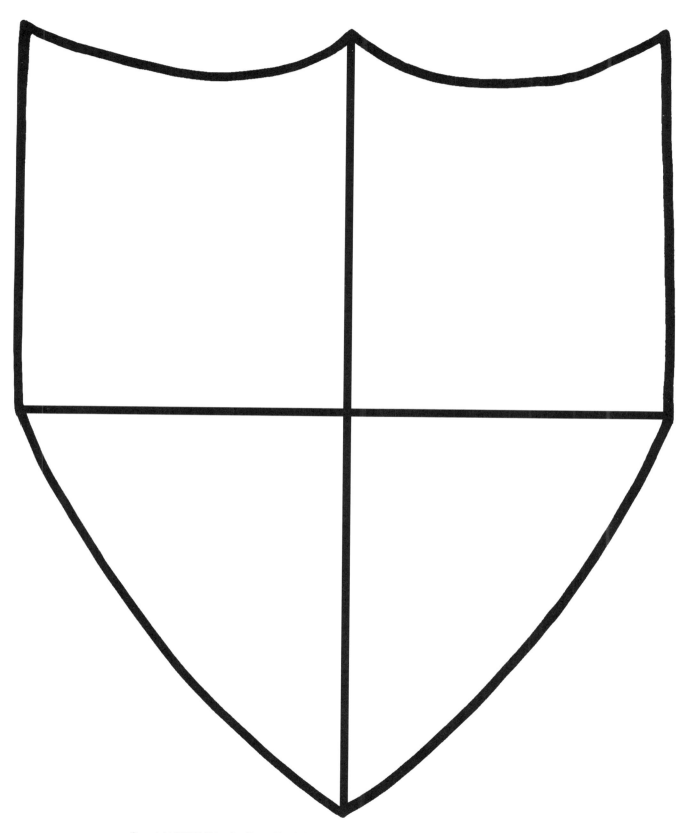

Simple Question #2: Who Am I?

Our Affirmation

I am a child of God.

God created me in God's image.

I am worthwhile.

I am loved.

Three Simple Questions to Help Children Know God

Quilt Square

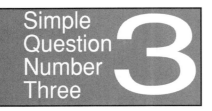

Who Are We Together?

First Week: The Family of God

Second Week: Followers of Jesus

Objectives

The children will

- discover that God is love;
- learn that as Christians we come to know God through the life and teachings of Jesus;
- recognize that because God loves us, we should love one another.

Bible Story

Week 1: Acts 10:34-36: Jesus is Lord of all.

Week 2: Luke 5:1-11, 27-32; 6:12-12: Jesus calls disciples.

Bible Verse

Galatians 3:26: You are all God's children through faith in Christ Jesus.

Focus for the Teacher

The Third Question

To answer the "Who are we together?" question, we must first recognize that we all are members of the human race. Scientific evidence even suggests that every human shares DNA with every other human. All people on the earth are one family.

Rueben Job looks at this truth and what it means to us in *Three Simple Questions*: "This makes each of us a member of this extended human family of God. God loves us as though each one of us was the only child of God in the world, just as God loves every other human being on the face of the earth. From Genesis to the Psalms and Prophets to the Gospels and Letters, the Bible reinforces this truth that Jesus taught and lived. To turn away from any of God's children is to turn away from God, who resides within, sustains, and loves each one beyond our comprehension, just as God loves us."

The Family of God

In the early days of the Christian movement, Peter wrestled with the question of who is eligible to join the faith family. The foundation for Peter's dilemma begins with the relationship between the Jews and the Gentiles (everyone who was not Jewish). According to Jewish law, the Jews were required to remain separate from the Gentiles, having only limited association with them. Because the earliest followers of Jesus were Jewish, it became standard operating procedure for a convert to become Jewish first and then to become Christian. As more and more Gentiles were converted to the faith, the debate over this double conversion grew. Was it truly necessary?

The event that answers this question occurred in Joppa. Joppa is a coastal city not far from Caesarea. Roman soldiers were stationed at Caesarea, a thriving seaport. Living and working in this area exposed people to a variety of cultures. Cornelius, a Roman official, was a Gentile God-fearer. God-fearers were those Gentiles who participated in the prayers of the synagogue and gave to the poor, but had not converted to Judaism.

One day, at three o'clock in the afternoon, Cornelius had a vision and was told to send for Peter. While Cornelius' servants were traveling, Peter went to the roof of the house where he was staying and also had a vision. In this vision a sheet filled with animals was being lowered to earth by its four corners. In the vision God told Peter to eat unclean animals that Jews were forbidden to eat. Peter was bewildered by this vision until Cornelius' servants arrived.

Peter went to Cornelius' home. Peter said, "You all realize that it is forbidden for a Jew to associate or visit with outsiders. However, God has shown me that I should never call a person impure or unclean" (Acts 10:28). As a result the first barriers between Jews and Gentiles came down. God doesn't show partiality to one group of people over another. Much to our surprise, God invites all to hear, receive, believe, and practice the good news. The message is clear: God's love is for everyone.

The Family of God for Children

How does this relate to our children? God loves each child equally. This includes the children in your class, the class bully that no one likes, the child who doesn't always take a bath, the child who is always getting into trouble, and the child whose parents do not live together. We might not label these persons as unclean, but sometimes our attitudes reflect this notion. Again, the message is clear: God's love is for everyone.

Followers of Jesus

Jesus invited the fishermen to "Come, follow me" (Matthew 4:19). Jesus also invites us. How we choose to respond to this invitation helps us discover that God is love, that God is revealed by Jesus, and that we all are God's children.

In Matthew 4:18-22 Jesus, the teacher, begins to gather disciples. A teacher gathering disciples around him was not unusual in Jesus' day. In fact, this was a way of life that received great respect in the community. Disciples would spend years with a teacher and, through discourse and discussion, they would learn. But Jesus' disciples were somewhat unorthodox. Sometimes a teacher would discover an especially bright student and would make arrangements for that student to be a disciple. Often the arrangement was initiated by the student asking the teacher for the honor of studying under the teacher. But when it came to Jesus, he was not only the one who did the choosing and calling of disciples, but also he looked in an unorthodox place (the workplace) and asked men who had shown no prior interest in spending their days in intellectual pursuits.

> God doesn't show partiality to one group of people over another. Much to our surprise, God invites all to hear, receive, believe, and practice the good news.
>
> — Rueben P. Job

The choosing of Simon to be Jesus' first disciple is significant. Simon, whose name was changed to Peter, the "rock," became the very foundation of the church. Peter's brother, Andrew, was also called to be a disciple.

Interestingly Jesus' very next choice was another set of brothers: James and John. There is some speculation that because they were named in the Gospels as the sons of Zebedee that perhaps their father was of some importance in the early church. We are not given any reason why these men decided to follow Jesus. But whatever the reason, they followed him without question.

Children as Followers of Jesus

Children may wonder how they can "follow" Jesus. They can't leave their parents and travel around the countryside as the early disciples did. But they can live as Jesus taught and tell the story of Jesus to others.

Living as Jesus taught means loving God and loving others, treating others as you want to be treated, worshiping God through prayer and praise, and serving God by serving others. These are all things that children can do—they just need the opportunity and encouragement to practice these actions in age-appropriate ways. As a teacher you can be instrumental in offering these opportunities. Thank you for what you do to help children become followers of Jesus.

Gather to Explore

Be sure that adult leaders are waiting when the first child arrives. Greet and welcome each child and involve him or her in an activity that introduces the theme for the day's activities.

Our Families

- As the children arrive, give each child a people figure to represent each person in his or her family. Instruct the children to cut out the figures. Precut the figures for younger children.

- Ask each child to decorate the figures to represent each member of her or his family.

- Encourage each child to tell you about his or her family.

- Help each child glue the correct number of people cutouts in a line next to his or her name, one for each family member.

- Help children compare the sizes of their families. Point out which families are different and which families are the same.

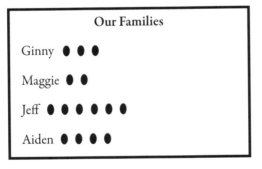

Prepare

✓ Photocopy the people figures (page 45). You will need one figure for each person in each child's family. Cut out the figures for younger children.

✓ Provide poster board, crayons or markers, glue, and safety scissors.

✓ Make a graph using the poster board. Write each child's name down one side of the poster board. Leave enough space for each child to glue his or her family figures in a line beside her or his name. See example to the left.

Family Quilt

- Give each child a quilt square.
- *Ask:* What are some things you like to do with your family?
- Encourage the children to draw pictures of their family in the style of a family portrait or to draw pictures of their family doing an activity they like to do together.
- Display the quilt squares around the room.
- *Say:* Today we are going to talk about a special family. We're going to talk about the family of God.

Prepare

✓ Photocopy and cut out a quilt square (page 45) for each child.

✓ Provide crayons or colored pencils.

FOG Buttons

- Children will design buttons with the letters FOG in the center. The letters stand for *Family of God*.

- Give each child at least two copies of the button circle to decorate with fine-tipped markers.

- Children should trace their circles onto poster board. If necessary, help them cut out the circles.

- Instruct the children to glue their decorated paper buttons onto the poster-board circles.

- Finally, give the children pin backs to glue on the backs of the buttons.

- Set the buttons aside to use during the *Celebrate and Praise God* section.

- *Say*: We have been talking about our families. The letters FOG are on our buttons. Can you guess what the letters stand for? (Let the children guess.) They stand for the *Family of God*. Because we are all God's children, we all are part of the family of God.

Prepare

✓ Photocopy and cut apart the "FOG Buttons" (page 60). You will need at least two for each child.

✓ Provide pin backs (available at craft stores), poster board, pencils, safety scissors, glue, and fine-tipped markers.

Our Family Tree

- Encourage the children to help you construct a family tree. Show the children the tree trunk you have mounted on a bulletin board or drawn on poster board.

- Give the children the brown paper you have prepared. Show the children how to twist the paper into narrow lengths.

- Use staples or glue to attach the brown lengths to make branches growing from the tree trunk.

- Hand out green construction paper and encourage children to help one another trace their handprints onto the paper and then cut out the handprints.

- Each child should write his or her name on a handprint and attach to the tree.

- **Option:** If you are a smaller church and have a pictorial directory available, use this alternative activity with the tree trunk and branches.

- Cut out all the pictures from the directory.

- Provide precut leaves or ask the children to cut out leaf shapes using the green construction paper.

- Instruct children to glue the pictures onto the leaves, then attach the leaves to the tree.

- *Say*: This is our family of God tree. Because we are all God's children, everyone at our church is part of the family of God.

Prepare

✓ Provide brown construction paper or paper rectangles cut from brown paper grocery bags, green construction paper, safety scissors, crayons or markers, stapler and staples or glue, and a bulletin board or poster board.

✓ Cut a tree trunk out of brown paper and mount it on a bulletin board. Or draw a simple tree trunk on poster board.

✓ **Option:** Provide a pictorial directory and precut leaves.

Look in the Bible

The Bible helps us discover the answers to the three simple questions.

Find Your Family

- Choose two children to be group leaders. Ask the two leaders to cover their eyes or to leave the room with another adult.

- Instruct the remaining children to find a safe hiding place in the room.

- Invite the group leaders back into the room or tell them to uncover their eyes.

- Encourage the two leaders to search for the hiding children. When a leader finds someone, that person comes out of hiding and clasps hands with the leader to make a "family." The "family" then moves together to find more children to add to their family.

- Continue until all the children have been found and added to one of the two family groups.

- Ask the two family groups to sit together and decide on a family name.

- Encourage the leader in each group to introduce her or his family to the other group.

- *Say*: Each group became a pretend family in this activity. Today we're talking about a real family that is very special. We're talking about the family of God. Everyone can be part of the family of God.

Fun With Scripture

- Instruct each family group to form a circle.

- Say today's Bible verse for the children: "You are all God's children through faith in Christ Jesus" (Galatians 3:26). Encourage the children to repeat the Bible verse.

- *Say*: Our Bible verse tells us that we all are God's children because we follow Jesus. Everyone who follows Jesus is part of the family of God.

- Give each circle a ball.

- *Say*: Toss these balls back and forth across the circle. Each time you catch a ball, shout out the Bible verse.

- After several minutes, ask the two circles to join in making one big circle.

- Tell the children to continue tossing both balls. When two children catch the balls at the same time, both children should shout out the Bible verse.

Prepare

✓ Provide two soft balls.

God Treats Everyone the Same

- Ask the children to move to the side of the room with the "Caesarea" sign. Invite the person playing the part of Cornelius to come in and tell the children Cornelius' part of the story.

- Instruct the children to move to the side of the room with the "Joppa" sign. Invite the person playing the part of Peter to come in and tell the children Peter's part of the story.

- Move the children back to Caesarea. Ask Cornelius and Peter to finish telling the story.

- If you choose not to use storytellers, tell the story yourself. Change something about yourself or your clothes when you tell each side of the story. You might wear a costume helmet for Cornelius and a Bibletimes headcovering for Peter. You might wear a nametag that says Cornelius and then change it to a nametag that says Peter. Or, you might wear two different cloak costumes.

- *Ask*: What did Peter see in his dream? (*a sheet being lowered from heaven with all kinds of animals on it*) What did God tell Peter? (*There is no such thing as "clean" and "unclean," and the creatures God created are all acceptable for food.*) What did Peter discover his dream meant for followers of Jesus? (*God treats everyone the same.*) What does Peter's dream say about who is part of the family of God? (*everyone*)

Prepare

✓ Photocopy "God Treats Everyone the Same" (page 61) for each actor.

✓ Invite a guest to portray Cornelius and another guest to portray Peter. Give each guest the script ahead of time.

✓ Photocopy and cut out the "Caesarea" and "Joppa" signs (pages 60 and 61).

✓ Provide scissors and any costume items for the visiting actors.

✓ Post the "Caesarea" and "Joppa" signs on opposite sides of the meeting space.

Who's in the Family of God?

- Line up chairs in the center of the room for a game of musical chairs, using one less chair then the number of children playing the game. Play the music while children walk around the chairs. Stop the music and let the children scramble for the chairs. One child will be left standing.

- *Say*: Wait a minute. Let's play this game as if we are the family of God.

- Place a single chair in the middle of an open area of the room. Tape a "Child of God" card on the back of the chair. Ask the children to form a circle around the chair.

- Play the music as children walk in a circle around the chair. Then stop the music. Explain that everyone must touch the chair in some way.

- Now add a second chair with a "Child of God" card taped to the back. Start the music again and ask the children to circle the chairs.

- Stop the music. Again, everyone must touch either chair in some way. Now add another chair and sign and continue play until there is a chair for every child in the group.

- *Ask*: What happened in this game that doesn't usually happen in most games? (*No one was left out.*)

- *Say*: God loves everyone. No one is left out of the family of God.

Prepare

✓ Photocopy and cut out a "Child of God" sign (page 60) for each child.

✓ Provide chairs (one per child), CD of lively music, CD player, and tape.

A Simple Practice

Discover ways to put into practice what you and the children have learned about being part of the family of God. Choose ways that match the children's interests and the time and resources you have available.

No Matter Who

- *Say*: I wonder who belongs in the family of God? Do you think a movie star belongs in the family of God? What about a football player? Of course they do! Let's play a game to guess who belongs to the family of God.

- Stand on one side of the room. Instruct the children to line up on the opposite side of the room. At your signal, the first player should run to you.

- Whisper in the player's ear a name from the list in the margin. The player returns to the group moving in a way that reflects the person named.

- The group tries to guess who the player was imitating.

- *Say*: The Bible story about Peter and Cornelius teaches us that God loves everyone. Everyone is included in the family of God—no matter who they are.

In or Out?

- *Say*: The Bible story about Peter and Cornelius teaches us that God loves everyone. Everyone is included in the family of God—even kids. Let's think about how we choose our friends.

- Give each child a piece of paper, a crayon, people figures, and safety scissors. Ask each child to cut out five people figures.

- Instruct each child to draw a large circle on her or his blank paper.

- *Say*: I'm going to name some kids we might meet as we go to school or church. If you think you would want this kid to play with you and be your friend, place one of your people figures inside the circle. If you think you would not want this kid to play with you and be your friend, place the people figure outside the circle. Be honest! This will help us think about how we include other kids in our own circle of friends. We will not show one another our papers.

- Read aloud the following statements and encourage the children to place their people figures inside or outside of their circles.

      a new kid in the neighborhood
      a kid from a different church
      a kid in a wheelchair
      a kid with a different skin color than mine
      a kid who lives in a poor part of town

- Ask the children to keep their paper circles in front of them and to leave their figures in place for use in the next activity.

Name List

skater
basketball player
soccer player
baby
grandmother
fashion model
singer
guitar player
preacher
teacher
photographer
homeless person

Prepare

✓ Photocopy the people figures (page 45). Each child will need five. Precut the figures for younger children.

✓ Provide blank paper, crayons, and safety scissors.

Celebrate and Praise God

One way we help children know that they are part of the family of God is to offer them opportunities to worship and praise both as a group and individually.

Prayers for the Family of God

- Remind children to keep their circle pages in front of them without moving their figures.

- *Say*: Our Bible story today reminds us that God loves everyone. Because God loves everyone, we're going to pray for the kids we placed in or out of our circles. This time when I name a kid, move the figure into your circle and say the words, "God, we welcome these kids into the family of God."

- *Pray*: God, we know that you love everyone. Help us show love as we welcome others into the family of God.

    We pray for new kids that move into our neighborhoods.
    God, we welcome these kids into the family of God.
    We pray for kids that go to different churches.
    God, we welcome these kids into the family of God.
    We pray for kids that have to use wheelchairs.
    God, we welcome these kids into the family of God.
    We pray for kids who have skin colors different from our own.
    God, we welcome these kids into the family of God.
    We pray for kids who live in the poor sections of town.
    God, we welcome these kids into the family of God.
    Amen.

Prepare

✓ Provide the people figures and circles used in the previous activity.

Button, Button, Who's Got the Button?

- Ask the children to form a circle.

- *Say*: We all are part of the family of God. Name a child and ask him or her to step into the center of the circle. Give the child a FOG button and say, "(*Name of child*), you are God's child, a special member of the family of God."

- Encourage all the children to clap and cheer for the child.

- Ask the child to step back into the circle and repeat the activity with another child. Continue until every child has received a FOG button.

- *Say*: You know you are part of the family of God, and now you can help someone else know that he or she is also part of the family of God. Take an extra FOG button. Give it to a friend or family member and explain that FOG stands for *Family of God*. Remind this person that she or he is part of God's family.

- *Pray*: Loving God, thank you for making us part of your special family. Help us to include others in your family by showing them love and care. Amen.

Prepare

✓ Provide the FOG buttons made earlier.

Second Week: Followers of Jesus

Gather to Explore

Be sure that adult leaders are waiting when the first child arrives. Greet and welcome each child and involve him or her in an activity that introduces the theme for the day's activities. The "Footprint Followers" faces are used in A Simple Practice.

Prepare a Bible Verse Game

- Place eleven copies of the footprint on a table or the floor.

- Write out the Bible verse on a markerboard or paper for the children to copy: "You are all God's children through faith in Christ Jesus" (Galatians 3:26).

- As the children arrive, assign each child one word of the Bible verse. Ask the child to write that word on a footprint. The reference is counted as one word.

- When the children have finished writing on the footprints, encourage them to put the Bible verse in correct order to check their work.

- *Say*: Our Bible verse tells us that, because we believe in Jesus, we are God's children. Today we will learn that as God's children we are also followers of Jesus.

- Set the footprints aside to use later in the lesson. If you have a large group of children, prepare more than one set of footprints.

Prepare

✓ Photocopy and cut out eleven "Footprints" (page 64).

✓ Provide markers and paper or a markerboard.

Name the Twelve

- Give each child the word puzzle and a pencil.

- *Say*: Jesus called twelve men to follow him and be his disciples. We know that four of the men were fishermen and that one was a tax collector. We know a lot about some of the disciples and hardly anything about others. We do know all of their names.

- Encourage the children to find the names of Jesus' twelve disciples. Instruct the children to look up Mark 3:16-17 in their Bibles to find a list of the names. (*James; John; Andrew; Peter; Matthew; Judas; Bartholomew; Thaddaeus; Philip; Thomas; Simon; and James, son of Alphaeus*)

- Remind the children that the first four disciples were fishermen. Ask them to count how many times the word *fish* is included in the puzzle.

Prepare

✓ Photocopy the "Find the Twelve" word puzzle (page 62) for each child.

✓ Provide pencils and Bibles.

Three Simple Questions to Help Children Know God

Footprint Followers

- Give each child a footprint to cut out. Precut the footprints for younger children.

- Encourage the children to make the footprints into a likeness of their faces. They may use crayons or markers to draw facial features and glue pieces of yarn to the top of the footprints for hair.

- *Say*: Jesus called disciples to follow him. Jesus also wants us to follow him. Our footprints can remind us that we are followers of Jesus.

- Set the footprints aside to use later in the lesson.

Footprint Invitations

- Give each child the "Follow Me" invitation insert and a piece of construction paper. Read the inserts to the children. Encourage the children to decorate the inserts with crayons or markers.

- Ask the children to fold the construction paper in half like a card and to glue the inserts inside the cards.

- Remind each child to sign her or his name to the invitation.

- *Say*: We're going to use this page to make invitations. You can invite friends and family to follow you to church. Since we're talking about following, I want you to follow my directions to finish your invitations. We will use your hands to make footprints.

- Set out the nonpermanent ink pads or the paint pads.

- *Say*:
  1. Put on a paint smock.
  2. Place the card with the blank cover facing up.
  3. Fold one hand into a fist.
  4. Press the side of your fist onto the paint pad.
  5. Now press the side of your fist onto the front of the pad. This will make the sole of the footprint. You may make more than one print.
  7. Wash the ink or paint off your hand.
  8. Press your thumb onto the pad.
  9. Now press your thumb onto the top of the fist print in the big toe position. Do this for each fist print.
  10. Continue making prints with your four fingers to add the toes to the fist prints.
  11. Wash the ink off your fingers.
  12. Set aside the invitations to dry.

- Send the dried invitations home with the children. Encourage the children to give them to family members or friends.

Prepare

✓ Photocopy one of the "Footprints" (page 64) for each child.

✓ Provide safety scissors, crayons or markers, glue, and yarn in hair colors.

Prepare

✓ Cut out the "Follow Me" invitation insert (page 63). Add your church's address and phone number. Then photocopy the invitation for each child.

✓ Provide construction paper, glue, crayons or markers, handwashing supplies, paint smocks, nonpermanent ink pads or shallow trays, paper towels, and washable paint.

✓ Make paint pads by folding paper towels and placing them in the bottom of a shallow tray. Pour washable paint onto the paper towels.

Look in the Bible

The Bible helps us discover the answers to the three simple questions.

Follow the Leader

- Ask the children to sit in a circle, either in chairs or on the floor. Join the circle yourself and be the first leader.

- *Say*: Let's play a game to see how good you are at following. We will do motions in rhythm. I will be the leader. When I change to a new motion, change as quickly as you can, but stay in rhythm.

  After we have completed three or four different motions, I will call out one of your names. That person must take over being the leader and will change the motions in rhythm. We will try to follow those changes quickly. Then the leader will call out another name. We will continue until we all have had a turn at being the leader.

- Begin patting your hands on your knees in a steady rhythm. Once the class has picked up the rhythm, choose another motion (for example, pat your left chest with your right hand and then pat your knees again).

- Continue until every class member is following, then quickly change to a new motion, such as clapping your hands twice. Between each motion return to patting your knees.

- Try to lull the children into feeling complacent and then quickly change the motion when they are not watching carefully.

- When you think that the children are beginning to understand, call out a child's name and let him or her become the leader, while you continue to play.

- Give all the children the opportunity to be the leader.

- *Say*: Jesus chose twelve people to be his followers. Four of the people were fishermen. When Jesus asked the fishermen to follow him, they immediately left their fishing boats and went with Jesus.

- *Ask*: Do you think it was hard for the fishermen to leave the work they were used to doing to follow Jesus? How do you think they felt?

Calling All Disciples

- *Say*: Today's story is in the Gospels of Matthew, Mark, and Luke. We're going to look mostly at the verses in Luke.

- Instruct the children to find Luke 5:1-11, 27-32 and 6:12-16 in their Bibles.

- Ask for volunteers to read the parts of the four Readers and six Scripture Readers in "Calling All Disciples."

Prepare

✓ Provide Bibles.

✓ Photocopy "Calling All Disciples" (page 64) for each child.

- *Say*: The first twelve disciples are often called the apostles. We know a lot about some of the disciples and very little about others. We do know that when Jesus called them to follow him, they all dropped what they were doing and followed him.

- *Ask*: Why do you think the disciples dropped what they were doing and followed Jesus? How do you think you might have responded if Jesus had come to you and told you to drop everything and follow him?

Follow the Scripture

- Ask the children to line up on one side of the room.

- Place the Bible-verse-word footprints that the children made earlier in a pattern around the room, starting on the side of the room where the children are now standing. Secure the footprints with tape.

- *Say*: Our Scripture helps us remember that we are children of God because of our faith in Jesus. That makes us followers of Jesus.

- Ask each child to walk the path following the footprints and say the Bible verse.

- Instruct the children to line up again. This time ask the children to hop the footprint path while saying the Bible verse.

- Continue the game, changing the way the children move along the footprint path. Try to make the motions more and more complicated or strenuous so that it is harder to move and speak at the same time. Some suggested motions are: crab walk, walk backwards, hop on one foot, do jumping jacks, walk while holding your ankles, and so forth.

Prepare

✓ Provide the Bible-verse-word footprints made earlier and tape.

Interview Followers

- Pair up the children. Ask each pair to interview a member of your congregation.

- The children may think of their own questions or use the following suggestions.

  1. Are you a follower of Jesus?

  2. Why?

  3. What does it mean to you to follow Jesus?

  4. What are some things you do because you are a follower of Jesus?

- If possible, provide video cameras for the children to film the interviews. If cameras are not available, remind the children to take notes or ask the children to draw pictures of the persons they interviewed.

- Call on the pairs to share their interviews with the class.

Prepare

✓ **Optional:** Provide video cameras or pencils and paper or crayons and paper.

A Simple Practice

Discover ways to put into practice what you and the children have learned about God. Choose ways that match the children's interests and the time and resources you have available.

Who Is a Follower?

- *Ask*: What do you think it means to be a follower of Jesus? (*Let the children respond.*)

- *Say*: Help me complete this sentence: "A follower of Jesus is someone who ..."

- Encourage the children to respond. Record their responses on a markerboard or large sheet of paper. Be ready to include the following: A follower of Jesus is someone who loves God, loves others, prays, serves God, believes in Jesus, gives to people in need, tells others about Jesus, forgives, and reads the Bible.

- *Say*: Those are all good responses. But it takes more than words to be followers of Jesus. We must also act like followers of Jesus.

- *Ask*: What do we do to love God? to love others? to serve God?

Prepare
✓ Provide a markerboard or a large sheet of paper and a marker.

I Can Be a Follower

- Give each child his or her footprint face made earlier in the lesson.

- *Say*: Think about one thing you can do this week that will let people know that you are a follower of Jesus. Turn over your footprint face. Write what you will do on the blank side of the footprint.

- Encourage the children to be specific.

Prepare
✓ Provide the footprint faces from "Footprint Followers" made earlier (see page 55).
✓ Provide crayons or markers.

Following Jesus Today

- *Say*: Our actions show others that we are followers of Jesus. Listen as I read three very short stories. After each story, let's think about what the child in the story might do to act like a follower of Jesus.

   1. Alyssa's church is planning a mission trip to Haiti this year, but she is too young to go. What can she do? (*Pray.*)

   2. Logan grew several sizes during the past year. His spring clothing is too small, but it is still in good shape. What can Logan do? (*Donate the clothing to someone who needs it.*)

   3. Lily's next-door neighbor is very old. Because she uses a walker to move around, she doesn't go outside of her house much. What can Lily do? (*Visit her neighbor.*)

- Encourage the children to suggest several answers.

Celebrate and Praise God

One way we help children know that they are part of the family of God is to offer them opportunities to worship and praise both as a group and individually.

Follow Me

- *Ask*: What are the words Jesus used to invite the disciples to become his disciples? (*Follow me.*) What did they do? (*They left their work and followed Jesus.*) If Jesus were to say to you today, "Follow me," what would you do?

- Teach the children the American Sign Language for the words, "Jesus said, 'Follow me.'" (See below.)

- Ask the children to sit in a circle; then select one child to be the leader.

- The leader should move around the circle, stopping to tap one child on the shoulder and repeating the signs to that child.

- When a child is tapped and given the signs, he or she joins the leader in moving around the circle.

- The leader (and followers) continues moving around the circle, tapping children and signing until all are following the leader.

- Ask the leader to lead the children around the room to the worship area.

- *Say*: (*Child's name*), you are a follower of Jesus.

- Continue repeating the phrase until you have named each child as a follower of Jesus. If you have a large group of children, name two or three children at one time.

- *Say*: We all are followers of Jesus.

- *Pray*: Thank you, God, for Jesus. Help us to follow his example and live our lives so that others will know we are your children. Amen.

Child of God	Child of God
Caesarea	

Three Simple Questions to Help Children Know God

God Treats Everyone the Same

by Sharilyn S. Adair

Our story mentions two towns: One is called Caesarea and one is called Joppa. Our story begins in Caesarea. (*Ask the children to start at the "Caesarea" sign.*)

Cornelius lived in Caesarea. He was a leader of many soldiers. Most people did not like soldiers, but Cornelius was a very kind man. He gave money to poor people. He loved God, and he prayed to God. But Cornelius did not know about Jesus.

One day when Cornelius was praying, an angel came to him. "Cornelius," said the angel, "God is happy that you pray and give money to the poor. God wants you to send for a man who is staying at a house in Joppa. The man's name is Peter." Then the angel went away.

Cornelius called one of his soldiers and two other people who worked in his house. He told them what the angel had said. He asked them to go to Joppa to find the man called Peter and bring him back with them.

Now let's move to Joppa. (*Ask the children to move to the "Joppa" sign.*)

Peter was staying in the house of a friend. Peter was hungry, but the meal was not ready, so he decided to pray. While he was praying, Peter had a dream. In the dream God told him that all kinds of food are good to eat. Then God told him that three men were looking for him and he should go with them.

Cornelius' men arrived, and Peter went with them. They traveled for two days to reach Caesarea. Let's go back to Caesarea. (*Ask the children to move back to the "Caesarea" sign.*)

Usually Peter would not go inside the house of a Roman soldier. But Peter remembered his dream. All kinds of people are good, just as all kinds of food are good.

Peter said, "God has shown me that no people are God's favorites. God loves everyone."

Then Peter went into the house and told Cornelius and all the people in his house about Jesus.

—from *BibleZone 8 Preschool* © 1999 Abingdon Press

Joppa

Find the Twelve

P H I L I P Q W Z M K
E F I S H X J U D A S
T H A D D A E U S T X
E X F I S H F Z Q T Z
R J A M E S Q J V H K
B A R T H O L O M E W
J M X H Q Z F H V W F
F E X O K A Y N K F I
I S I M O N Y Q Z I S
S L V A N D R E W S H
H F I S H F I S H H Z

Three Simple Questions to Help Children Know God

Follow me to

church

address

worship times

Calling All Disciples

Reader 1: Jesus was the promised Messiah who God sent to help everyone.

Reader 2: But there was so much to do, and Jesus needed helpers.

Reader 3: He found his first four helpers by the lake.

Scripture Reader 1: Read Luke 5:1-4.

Scripture Reader 2: Read Luke 5:9-11.

Reader 4: Wow! They left everything and followed Jesus. That's some kind of faith.

Reader 1: Later Jesus saw a very unlikely helper, but that didn't stop Jesus.

Scripture Reader 4: Read Luke 5:27-28.

Reader 2: Levi also left everything.

Reader 3: Sometimes Levi is known as Matthew.

Reader 4: Other people had a hard time understanding why Jesus would even hang out with Matthew and his friends.

Reader 1: But Jesus explained.

Scripture Reader 5: Read Luke 5:29-32.

Reader 2: Sick people, not healthy ones, need a doctor; so Jesus did not come to invite good people to turn to God, but instead those who were sinners.

Reader 3: In the end Jesus called twelve to be his disciples or followers.

Scripture Reader 6: Read Luke 6:12-16.

Reader 4: So, the first twelve disciples, otherwise known as apostles, learned from Jesus and set an example for the rest of us.

—from *Rock Solid Older Elementary Mini* © 2008 Cokesbury.

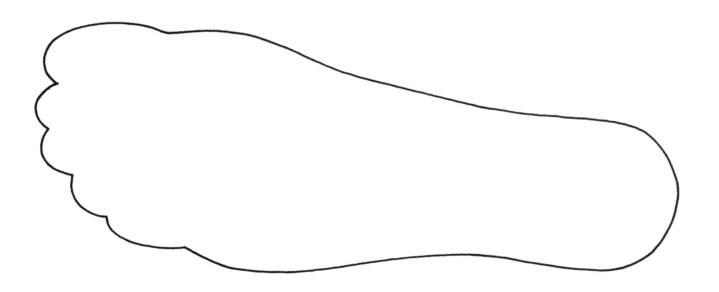

Three Simple Questions to Help Children Know God